The Everyday Guide to Primary Geography: Art

Margaret Mackintosh
and Gemma Kent
Series Editor: Julia Tanner

Series introduction

Geography is a vitally important component in a rich, broad and balanced primary curriculum. It is a subject which is driven by curiosity about the world as it is now and how it might change in the future. It provides the knowledge, understanding and skills necessary to address the great social, economic, environmental and ethical challenges which face humankind in the 21st century. It involves not only finding out where places are and what they are like, but also investigating how they have evolved and changed in the past, and how they may develop in the future. It enables children to make sense of places they know from first-hand experience, and of the wider world they have yet to explore. It helps them to understand their place in the world, and how people and places are linked at every level from local to global. It invites them to consider the impact of their actions on the environment, what they value locally and globally, and how they can contribute to the creation of a better future.

As series editor, I hope to inspire you to engage in active 'curriculum making' by providing stimulating ideas which you can adapt, extend or modify to meet the needs and interest of your class and your school's curriculum. All the activities are tried and tested, demonstrating how everyday and easily accessible resources, used creatively, can enhance and enrich pupils' geographical learning. Each double page is divided into panels with the key geographical learning opportunities on the left, supported by downloadable resources available from the webpage for this Guide (see below).

High-quality geographical work incorporates three key interrelated elements (Table 1). The first of these is an enquiry approach that involves asking geographical questions and using a range of skills, some specifically geographical, to find the answers. The second is the study of places, such as the local area, town, region, country or, at a global scale, continent, or the whole world. The third element involves learning about the physical and/or human and/or environmental geography of the places studied. Combining these different elements can enable pupils to think geographically in authentic learning activities which have real purposes, audiences and outcomes.

Enquiry, geographical skills and fieldwork	Asking and answering questions Planning and undertaking geographical enquiries Communicating the outcome of enquiries Making and using maps Using globes, atlases and digital mapping Fieldwork skills Using secondary resources such as books, websites and images Understanding differing points of view
Studying places – place and locational knowledge	The school grounds and local area The UK, Europe and the wider world Localities in the UK, Europe and the wider world Locational knowledge
Physical, human and environmental geography	**Physical geography** • landscapes, volcanoes, rivers, coasts • the weather, seasons and climate • landscapes, plants and animals **Human geography** • homes, buildings, villages, towns and cities • journeys and the movement of people, goods and ideas • jobs, agriculture, fishing, mining, manufacturing, transport, services • land use and the location of activities **Environmental geography** • change and development • caring for the environment and the planet • sustainability and environmental responsibility

Table 1: The three elements in high-quality geographical work

This series illustrates the amazing scope of geography in the primary curriculum, and the stimulating range of learning approaches it encompasses. It showcases high-quality geographical work contributed by primary classes in the UK and beyond. I hope it will be an inspiration to you to create challenging, exciting and satisfying geographical learning experiences for the children you teach.

Julia Tanner, June 2014

Resources to accompany this Guide, such as activity sheets, teacher guidance, extra activities and cross-curricular links, are available to download from the Geographical Association website.
Go to **www.geography.org.uk/everydayguides**
Click on the button for this Guide and then enter the password **MK14LD**

Contents

Geography through art 4

The Block by Romare Bearden 6
Investigate local houses and buildings

Rush Hour by George Segal 8
Investigate your local area and urban landscapes

Winter Tunnel with Snow, March, 2006 by David Hockney 10
Rural landscapes and seasonal change

Adire cloth by the Yoruba women of Nigeria 12
The clothes we wear and where they come from

Riverside Museum, Glasgow by Dame Zaha Hadid 14
Iconic buildings – their design, function and location

The Nenets of Northern Siberia by Sebastião Salgado 16
Landscapes, weather and life in Polar regions

175 The Almost Circle by Friedensreich Hundertwasser 18
Settlement patterns, land use and routes

Red Slate Line by Richard Long 20
Physical landscapes, rocks and land art

Day and Night by Maurits Cornelis Escher 22
Lines of latitude, time zones and seasonal change

Cattle Market, Braintree, Essex, 1937 by Edward Bawden 24
Food production and distribution

Paintings of London and Venice by Canaletto and Monet 26
London and Venice, waterways in cities

Surprised! (or Tiger in a Tropical Storm) by Henri Rousseau 28
Tropical rainforests, biodiversity and deforestation

Cotopaxi, Ecuador by the Quechuan people of Ecuador 30
Volcanoes, mountains and life in a village in Ecuador, South America

London Underground Map by Harry Beck 32
Maps as art forms and ways to communicate spatial information

Northumberlandia, the Lady of the North by Charles Jencks 34
The creation, destruction and management of landscapes, including National Parks

Useful resources and websites 36

Geography through art

This Guide is about the use of works of art to stimulate, enliven and enrich geography teaching and learning at key stages 1 and 2. It presents a wide range of classroom strategies for using art to develop pupils' geographical thinking, knowledge and understanding, and to extend their geographical skills. It also explores the rich possibilities for cross-curricular work through linking geography with art and other subjects.

The aims of the Guide are to:
- demonstrate the value of art as a stimulus for promoting geographical thinking and language
- exemplify strategies for developing geographical skills such as enquiry, map work, fieldwork and visual literacy through all kinds of artworks
- illustrate creative ideas for enhancing pupils' knowledge and understanding of places, physical, human and environmental geography, and their locational knowledge through art
- provide valuable ideas and resources to use in and beyond the classroom.

The value of art

Investigating art works enables pupils to understand that different people see, interpret and represent the world around them in different ways. Throughout history, artists have been inspired by places. They have utilised a plethora of media to create sketches, paintings, prints, collages, embroideries, textiles, ceramics and sculptures to either represent or convey the spirit of a particular place or express their emotional reaction to it. Art works can provoke strong emotional responses: evoking a sense of wonder at the beauty of nature, of awe at the power of an erupting volcano, or of desolation at the extent of urban decay

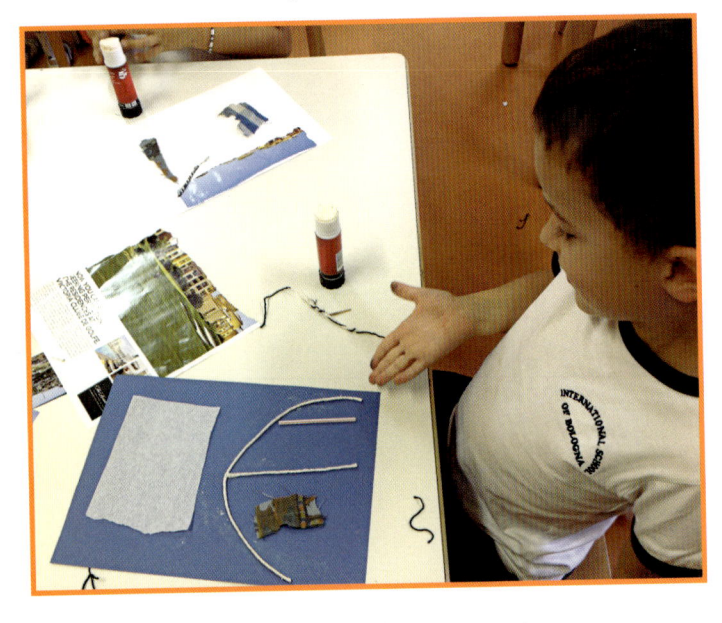

As they mature, pupils can move from straightforward questioning of an artwork (e.g. What does it show? What does it tell us about the place?) to more sophisticated discussions on how and why the artwork was created, and what impression of the place the artist wished to convey. They develop critical skills in visual literacy, including the ability to make sense of visual images and to understand that often those images are created with a particular purpose and audience in mind.

Visual literacy is a core skill in primary geography, which is essentially a visual subject. When teaching geography we try to give pupils as much visual, practical fieldwork experience as possible. If fieldwork is not possible, we frequently substitute photographs as the next best thing. Yet, the artist David Hockney is convinced that 'in the West we have been over-conditioned by the camera's way of seeing, and that this has severely limited our engagement with the world and the ways in which our experience of that world can be reshaped pictorially' (Livingstone, 2012). Here, Hockney invites us to go beyond photographs, to explore more widely the images of the world we construct in our minds and to express them by making art in many forms (including painting, sculpture and land art) and for a range of audiences.

Echoing Hockney's sentiments, John Berger observes: 'To look is an act of choice… We never look at just one thing: we are always looking at the relation between things and ourselves… The photographer's way of seeing is reflected in his [sic] choice of subject, the painter's way of seeing is reconstituted by the marks he makes on canvas or paper, yet, although every image embodies a way of seeing, our perception or appreciation of an image depends also upon our own way of seeing' (1972). Hockney and Berger's views encapsulate the thinking behind this book. We would like to reshape pupils' worlds pictorially, enable them to go beyond just photographs. We believe that in encountering the work of artists and designers pupils can discover their own way of seeing and experiencing. After all, enhancing pupils' engagement with their world is where art and geography meet.

Art in its myriad forms

We have taken a broad view of art to include painting, photography, collage, architecture, sculpture, textiles, land art (large and small), graphics, linocut and lithograph. Specific examples of these different media are included as much for their own sake, as for that artist's way of seeing and experiencing the world. We have chosen particular art forms with the intention that each one enables us to focus on a different aspect of geography, these include:

- **architecture:** three-dimensional functional structures designed for a specific purpose allow a focus on buildings
- **photography:** black and white art images provide us with a different interpretation from full-coloured ones
- **graphic:** intricate works where the emphasis is on representing detail of our real or an imagined world
- **maps:** artworks that convey to us the skilful representation and communication of spatial information
- **land art:** involves us in the aesthetics of enhancing or reshaping of natural and worked landscapes
- **woodcut and lithograph:** forms that emphasise to us the power of print-based imagery
- **paintings and collages:** imaginative, realist, impressionist and indigenous artworks provide us with different ways of seeing places
- **sculpture:** tactile, three-dimensional forms offer us a variety of perspectives
- **textile:** art-based, functional items allow us to develop an appreciation of craft skills.

Why use art in geography?

Linking works of art with geography invites pupils to explore different 'ways of seeing' and to consider how artists represent the world. Working with a wide variety of art forms demonstrates different artists' perspectives and interpretations of the world, and encourages pupils to:

- talk, discuss and develop a critical vocabulary and sense of judgement about art, geography and the world around them
- discover that it is safe to express opinion, emotion and feeling in art and geography
- appreciate that different people have different opinions about art, geography and their world
- become aware of the qualities of art and design, leading them to look for, recognise and appreciate beauty in urban and rural landscapes
- develop a positive attitude towards being adventurous and experimental in creating their own art in geography
- become confident in representing ideas and information pictorially
- develop their sensitivity towards the world around them, its aesthetics, beauty and eyesores
- learn that human actions can enhance and damage the aesthetics of their world.

Using this guide

This Guide has been written for those who work, or hope to work, with pupils in primary schools, including those with geography leadership roles, with responsibility for whole-curriculum planning and/or the quality of teaching and learning. The Guide will be of interest to educators, to anyone excited by holistic and creative approaches, and to those who believe that primary pupils learn best when they are introduced to, stimulated by and motivated by engaging and challenging activities.

Fifteen very different types of art feature in this Guide. Each double-page spread provides brief information about the work of art and the artist, outlines ideas for sharing the work with pupils and offers an associated art activity. Next, a series of geographical activities are given together with details of the geographical potential developed using that particular work of art as a stimulus. An accompanying webpage provides cross-curricular links and resources, including web addresses where images of the art works and extra material can be accessed.

The ideas we offer for using the art works are developed in approximate age range order, from key stage 1 through to upper key stage 2, but the majority can be adapted for use across the primary age range.

We hope this Guide will encourage teachers to explore and develop the full potential of a wide range of art genres as the stimulus for geographical work. We also hope it inspires teachers to be adventurous and creative as they experiment with ideas in their geography teaching.
(Mackintosh, 2013).

Web-based resources

Each double page spread has additional web-based resources. These include;

- key vocabulary
- cross-curricular links
- weblinks and resources
- activity sheets
- examples of pupils' work
- instructions
- additional activities

Go to www.geography.org.uk/everydayguides to download the resources.

References

Berger, J. (1972) *Ways of Seeing.* London: Penguin.

Livingstone, M. (2012) *David Hockney: A bigger picture.* London: Royal Academy of Arts.

Mackintosh, M. (2013) 'Representing places in maps and art' in Scoffham, S. (ed) *Teaching Geography Creatively.* Abingdon/New York: Routledge, pp. 74-84.

The Block
1971
created by Romare Bearden

Reproduced with permission © Romare Bearden Foundation/DACS, London/VAGA, New York 2013

This mixed-media collage depicts a street in Harlem, an area of New York, USA

Geographical enquiry and skills

- enquiry – asking and answering questions
- using geographical vocabulary
- using aerial photographs
- using and making maps
- fieldwork – making observations

Geographical knowledge and understanding

- place knowledge – the local area
- features of houses and other buildings
- features of the local area
- local facilities, such as shops, the doctors' surgery, the library and places of work

To access extra resources from the Everyday Guides web page, see page 2.

The Block is a 5.5m-long collage made using mixed media on hardboard. It consists of six panels (each 121.9 x 91.4cm), which, when displayed together, depict a row of houses in the Harlem district of New York. Romare Bearden (1911–1988) – an African-American artist and writer – was inspired to create *The Block* by the view from his window (see Everyday Guides webpage for Bearden's explanation). The collage can be used as a stimulus for investigating your local area, focusing on 'My street' or 'My neighbourhood'. It also provides an excellent starting point for investigating local buildings and facilities.

Sharing the painting

Display the collage and use prompts to encourage discussion. What do the pupils notice first about *The Block*? Draw their attention to the buildings and the people. What do they think the buildings are used for? What are the people doing? How is the scene similar to/different from their street? Is this a street they'd like to visit? Why/ why not? Read Bearden's quote on the inspiration for the collage, 'I was intrigued by the series of houses I could see from [the] windows. Their colors, their forms, and the lives they contained within their walls fascinated me' (see Everyday Guides webpage for the full quote), to establish that, although *The Block* was inspired by a street in New York it is also a work of his imagination.

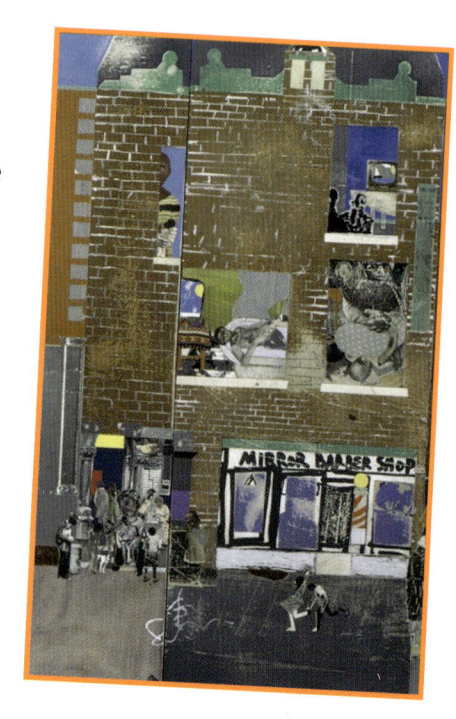

Teaching activities

Art activity

If there is a row of houses visible from your school, use this as inspiration for the activity. If not, as a class visit a street near to the school and ask the pupils to photograph or sketch what they see. Explain that they are to create a Bearden-style class collage of the street. Encourage them to look carefully at fixed features, such as buildings and trees, as well as people, animals and traffic.

Back in the classroom, the pupils should sketch their ideas first. Draw their attention to the range of materials and techniques Bearden employed to create *The Block* (including cut and pasted printed, coloured and metallic papers, photocopies, pencil, ink marker, gouache, watercolour and pen and ink on Masonite (hardboard)). Provide a wide range of materials to encourage pupil creativity in representing the street and buildings.

Model houses

Identify a street with a variety of houses in your local area. Visit it and encourage the pupils to identify the different types of houses (e.g. detached/semi-detached/terraced houses, bungalows, block of flats) and to note specific features (e.g. number and position of windows, doors, whether the house has a porch, the types of building materials used). Use geographical vocabulary to name and describe what pupils see. Ask pairs of pupils to photograph and record information about one house.

Back at school invite the class to create a model of the street. Each pair of pupils should use the information they collected to create an accurate model of the house they studied. Once the houses are complete, assemble the model street. Encourage pupils to play with the model using small-world people and animals.

Aerial photographs and maps

Talk about the similarities and differences between maps and aerial views. Study a large-scale OS map (either 1:1250 or 1:2500) of the street the pupils modelled and identify the individual buildings. Discuss how houses and other buildings appear as a different shape when seen from above. Ask pupils what shapes they think the buildings or other features they saw might look like from above. Demonstrate an aerial view either by 'flying' a toy or puppet bird over the model; or by looking at the street on Google Earth. What might the bird see? What can pupils see? How is this different from what is shown on the large-scale OS map? Invite pupils to make their own map of the street, using a simple key.

Local buildings and landmarks

Take the pupils on a walk around the local area to look at local landmarks and important buildings or features (these might include shops, places of work, playgrounds, places of worship, doctors' surgery, bus stops, swimming pool or leisure centre). Encourage pupils to observe and name the physical and human geographical features they see. Take photographs of significant buildings and landmarks.

Back in the classroom, share the photographs of the local area. Can the pupils describe where each building/landmark/feature is? Support pupils in using appropriate locational language, for example: 'The police station is next to the playground', 'The park is opposite our school', 'The bus stop is by the shops', and so on (see Everyday Guides webpage for further suggestions). As a class, add the photos to a pre-drawn large-scale base map of a section of the local area.

Ask pupils how they feel when moving around the local area. Where is their favourite place? Which places are their least favourite? Provide pupils with sticky notes on which to draw smiley or sad faces then invite them to place the faces on the map and explain their choices to the class.

Rush Hour
1987
created by George Segal

This bronze sculpture depicting a group of people stands in Finsbury Avenue Square in central London

Geographical enquiry and skills

- enquiry – asking and answering questions
- using geographical vocabulary to name human features of environment
- using directional and locational language
- using atlases, globes and wall maps

Geographical knowledge and understanding

- locational knowledge – countries to which pupils have travelled
- place knowledge – local area and region
- journeys in the local area
- different modes of transport for long and short journeys
- the effect of weather patterns on travel

To access extra resources from the Everyday Guides web page, see page 2.

George Segal (1924–2000) created his *Rush Hour* sculpture in 1983 (see Everyday Guides webpage for more details). It depicts a group of commuters. Pupils may be surprised that the Finsbury Avenue Square sculpture has been placed at street level in central London, and appears to mingle with the workers from the surrounding office buildings.

Rush Hour can act as a stimulus for investigating pupils' journeys. The accessibility of the sculpture, whether seen at first-hand or in a photograph, makes it a great springboard for discussing transport and journeys on local, national and global scales. The activities encourage pupils to think about their experiences of travel, as well as the relationships between the purpose and length of journeys and different modes of transport.

Sharing the sculpture

Display and discuss an image of *Rush Hour* (see Everyday Guides webpage for links). What do the pupils think it is? Who might the people be? Where are they going to/coming from? What is the place like? What clues can they see in the landscape? Explain that the London version of *Rush Hour* is near Liverpool Street Station. Can they say why the artist chose to put the sculpture there? Discuss the journeys the pupils make on foot, including to the park, to shops. Why do they make some journeys on foot? What journeys do they make by car, bus, train or plane? Why?

Teaching activities

Art activity

Ask the pupils to draw two self-portraits showing them walking to school: one in winter and the other in summer. Discuss similarities and differences. Encourage pupils to create a Plasticine or clay model from one of their self-portraits. Arrange the models into seasonal groups, as in *Rush Hour*.

Weather and travel

Look at images of *Rush Hour* and decide which season the sculpture is set in. Ask pupils to give reasons for their decision. Pupils could then think about how the artist, George Segal, might have designed *Rush Hour* for a different season, and draw, model or paint their alternative version.

Talk about the journeys pupils make in summer and in winter. Discuss the effect of the weather on journeys – how it affects their choice of clothing, mode of transport, and destination. Record any patterns pupils identify.

Gather images of travel problems caused by floods, snow, fog, ice, extreme heat, and so on. Use these as a stimulus for discussing the impact of extreme weather on journeys. Invite pupils to devise different travel scenarios in different types of weather then role play or use small-world models to enact the journey.

Journey role plays

Ask groups of pupils to simulate *Rush Hour*. They should pose as if making a specific journey – to/from school, the beach, the supermarket, to bed. As pupils take up a pose, use 'thought tracking': invite individuals to explain their thoughts or feelings aloud. Either tap each person on the shoulder, or hold a cardboard thought-bubble above their head. Develop this technique by asking pupils to act out journeys made by other people – e.g. an adult relative, a sibling or cousin. Prompt questions can include: Where are they? Where are they coming from/going to? What can they see? What is the weather like? How do they feel about their mode of transport? Are they enjoying their journey? What is their destination like?

Use a digital camera to record these 'living sculptures' – and print the images for pupils to annotate with comments in the form of speech/thought bubbles. Create your own *Rush Hour* gallery.

Our journeys

Collect information about the different journeys pupils make and how they make them. Discuss the number of pupils who have travelled by bus, train and airplane, for example. Use an appropriate geographical technique, such as a pictogram or bar graph, to present the information.

Where do pupils go on foot, by car, bus, bicycle, train and plane? Why? Encourage pupils to explain what influences the choice of transport. Discuss length of journey, safety, and such aspects as scenery. What countries have pupils visited? To help develop their locational knowledge, use a world map or globe to locate the places they mention. Record their journey information in terms of distance and direction from their home area. Use appropriate directional and locational vocabulary.

Extend pupils' locational knowledge of places around the world through role play. Set up a travel agency that sells tickets for a range of destinations and different modes of transport.

Winter Tunnel with Snow, March, 2006
painted by David Hockney

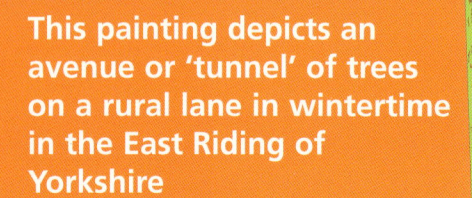

This painting depicts an avenue or 'tunnel' of trees on a rural lane in wintertime in the East Riding of Yorkshire

Geographical enquiry and skills

- enquiry – asking and answering questions
- using geographical vocabulary – to describe seasons, trees and change
- route finding on a map
- using and making maps
- visual literacy – using photographs to identify change
- fieldwork skills – observation and recording

Geographical knowledge and understanding

- locational knowledge – Yorkshire in the UK
- features of rural landscapes
- trees in the local environment
- weather and seasonal change

To access extra resources from the Everyday Guides web page, see page 2.

©David Hockney Photo credit: Richard Schmidt

David Hockney, one of the UK's greatest living artists, was born in Bradford in 1937. For some years Hockney lived and worked in the USA, but he now lives in Bridlington on the East Yorkshire coast. Like most artists, Hockney uses different media to create his artworks. As well as painting in oil and watercolour, he has painted electronically (using Brushes on an iPad); constructed photomontages from digital images; and used video to record the agricultural landscape near Bridlington. *Winter Tunnel with Snow, March, 2006*, is an ideal starting point for investigating landscapes, winter weather and seasonal change in rural areas. Together with his other Yorkshire-based landscapes, David Hockney's paintings act as a stimulus for fieldwork and mapping activities that involve pupils in looking at trees in the local area.

Sharing the painting

Display *Winter Tunnel with Snow, March, 2006* (see Everyday Guides webpage for links). What can the pupils see in the painting? Do they like it? Are there any surprises? Invite pupils to place themselves in the scene and lead into either a drama or movement activity, using prompts such as: What would it be like to walk along the avenue of trees? What would they have to wear? What would they be able to see, smell, hear, feel? Discover whether pupils know of, or have visited, a place like the Wolds in East Yorkshire. Would they like to visit the Winter Tunnel – why or why not? Would they like to be able to paint like David Hockney?

Teaching activities

Art activity

Either in the school grounds or a local park; encourage the pupils to study and draw or paint a tree *en plein air* (out of doors). Draw their attention to different types of tree and encourage them to notice differences between the trunk, bark, branches, silhouette and leaves of a variety of trees. If possible, revisit the trees each term to make rubbings of the bark and leaves, and to take photographs and/or paint season changes.

Trees and seasonal change

Painting both *en plein air* and from photographs, Hockney recorded the avenue or 'tunnel' of trees on Woldgate (an area between Bridlington and Kilham in East Yorkshire) throughout the four seasons. Display copies of all four paintings – *Late Spring Tunnel, May, 2006*; *Winter Tunnel, February, 2006*; *Early July Tunnel, 2006*; and *Early November Tunnel, 2006* – without titles. Do the pupils think all four paintings show the same location? Encourage them to describe similarities and differences. Can they match season to painting? Their explanations should lead in to the identification and discussion of seasonal changes; record key points from this discussion.

Provide copies of Hockney's *Three Trees near Thixendale, Winter 2007*; *Three Trees near Thixendale, Spring 2008*; *Three Trees near Thixendale, Summer 2007*; and *Three Trees near Thixendale, Autumn 2008* without captions and invite pupils to sequence the paintings by season. Discuss seasonal change in the agricultural activity in Thixendale. Look at images of the countryside in a range of books and discuss in which season each was taken. Ask pupils to choose spring, summer, autumn, or winter and draw or paint a picture of the countryside in that season. Can other pupils work out which season it depicts?

Maps from paintings

Locate Bridlington, Kilham and Woldgate on satellite images and draw pupils' attention to features of the rural landscape seen from above, especially the patchwork of fields.

Display Hockney's *Winter Tunnel with Snow, March, 2006* and invite pupils to imagine that they are in the painting. Explain that, as they walk along the avenue of trees they are to map the area shown in the painting (using the satellite image as reference) for other people 'visiting' the Winter Tunnel. This activity provides lots of useful information about the pupils' understanding of maps and map making. As their maps are based on a winter scene, pupils may include snow and footprints. Would they draw the same map from a summer painting? Discuss what information should and should not be included in a map. Can they provide a key for their map? What should be included in the key?

A local trees trail

With the class, identify a series of significant or distinctive trees near your school. (The presence of both evergreen and deciduous trees can provide a focus for extending the pupils' knowledge and understanding of trees and seasonal change.) Help pupils to plan and mark on an appropriate street map, a safe route from school to each of the trees in turn. Visit the trees and ask pupils to take digital images of each one. Mark the position of the trees on a street or large-scale OS map and ensure pupils use this to revisit the trees several times throughout the year to record seasonal change.

Without the pupils, visit each tree and photograph the bark, buds, leaves, blossom and fruit or berries. Provide a print of each picture and ask pupils to group together and then sequence the photographs by type of tree. Invite them to match the sets to their own tree photographs. Create a display showing 'Trees in our area' incorporating the maps and photos. Encourage pupils to add comments about what they have learned.

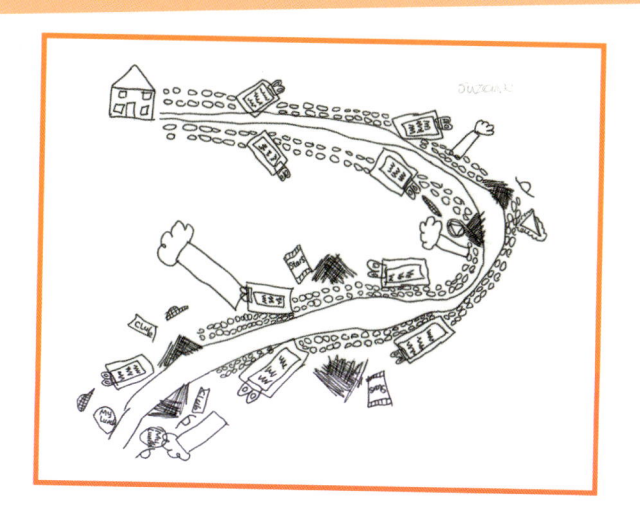

Adire Cloth
c. 1966
created by the Yoruba women of Nigeria

This textile art was created by the Yoruba women of south-east Nigeria. It is decorated with traditional ethnic patterns

Geographical enquiry and skills

- enquiry – asking and answering questions
- using geographical vocabulary – names of fibre-producing plants and animals
- collecting and communicating information
- using globes and wall maps

Geographical knowledge and understanding

- locational geography – location of the Equator, Tropics, Nigeria, Africa
- place knowledge of Abeokuta, and Nigeria
- weather and climate patterns
- how and where clothes are made
- human activity in production of fibres, textiles and clothing, from farmer to consumer
- international trade in clothing

To access extra resources from the Everyday Guides web page, see page 2.

Adire cloth is a resist-dyed textile. Yoruba women of Nigeria pass the skilled craft down through the generations. They create the patterns with cassava-starch paste, drawing them with fingers or sticks, or using stencils cut out by the men. The pasted cloth is dried in the sun before being dipped in a vat of indigo dye (obtained from plant leaves). The dye coats, rather than penetrates, the fabric where it is not protected by paste. The cloth emerges bright yellow, but changes to blue in contact with the air. Pieces of *Adire Cloth* (like this one, bought in Nsukka Market in Eastern Nigeria, see Everyday Guides webpage for a larger image) can act as the stimulus for an investigation of textiles, the types of textiles we wear and where our clothes come from. This type of textile may also be used to introduce pupils to the processes involved in using natural fibres to make clothes, and to the international trade in clothing.

Sharing the textile

Study the design panels in the *Adire Cloth*. How many different patterns are there? Explain that to the Yoruba each pattern has a particular meaning. What do the pupils think the patterns on this cloth might represent? How do they think the cloth is made? Describe the resist process: when the indigo dye is applied, it runs off the cassava-starch paste (used to create the design) like 'water off a duck's back', but the dye coats the exposed fabric. Once the fabric dries the paste is flaked or washed off the pattern emerges against a dark blue background. Challenge the pupils to identify and sequence all the stages needed to complete an *Adire Cloth*. Mention that this cloth consists of two panels stitched together, so that the designs are repeated on each half.

Teaching activities

Art activity

Make your own class *Adire Cloth*. Provide each pupil with a (15 x 15cm) square of light cotton fabric or sugar paper. Invite the pupils to design a pattern, preferably something with personal meaning, on scrap paper. Next, they use white wax crayons or a colourless candle to copy their design onto the fabric or sugar paper. Gently brush dark blue ink or thin paint all over the fabric/paper, and watch as the liquid runs off the waxed pattern, but colours the fabric/paper. Assemble the squares into a unique class *Adire Cloth*.

Create a textile book

Focus on textiles made from natural fibres. Have any of the pupils seen sheep being sheared? Or the spinning, weaving, knitting, felting or dyeing of wool, or printing on fabric? If possible invite experts to demonstrate and/or set up art and craft workshops in the school. Investigate and dramatise the spinning, weaving, knitting or felting processes – from producer to consumer. Show how animal or vegetable fibres are made into yarn which are then woven into textiles; include the dyeing and printing processes. As you demonstrate how these fabrics are made into the clothes we wear, emphasise that these traditional techniques are used less and that textiles are now made by machines in factories.

Use non-fiction books or the internet to investigate the sources of natural yarns, including wool, cotton, silk, linen, and possibly coconut and bamboo. Identify which originate from animals and which from plants and where they are farmed or grown. Pupils could create their own non-fiction book about the origins of textiles and how we use them illustrated with samples of the textiles.

Where did the Adire Cloth come from?

Identify where *Adire Cloth* originates. Locate the city of Abeokuta, the country Nigeria, and the continent Africa on a globe or wall map.

Demonstrate and explain the nesting arrangement: whereby the city nests inside the country, which, in turn, nests inside the continent. Once you have located the city, display a satellite image of Abeokuta and ask pupils what they can see. Can they identify roads, housing estates, hospitals, rivers? Pupils may be surprised at some of the names they encounter. Use weather forecasting websites to investigate the city's weather and climate, linking these to latitude (see Everyday Geography webpage for links). Use relevant geographical vocabulary including 'Tropics' and 'Equator'.

Where do our clothes come from?

Invite pupils to collect information from the labels in their clothes, including the composition of the textile and its country of origin. Discuss what textiles we wear and where our clothes come from. Either individually or as a class, pupils use appropriate methods, such as bar graphs and illustrated maps, to present and communicate the clothing label information. Identify which part of the world most of our clothes come from.

1. Africa (continent)
2. West Africa (region)
3. Nigeria (country)
4. Abeokuta (city)
5. Yoruba woman

©Joe Lodge (Creative commons licence)

Riverside Museum, Glasgow
2007
designed by Dame Zaha Hadid

This spectacular building stands on the banks of the River Clyde in Glasgow, Scotland, and was built to house a museum of transport and travel

Geographical enquiry and skills

- enquiry – asking and answering questions
- visual literacy – using and interpreting photographs
- fieldwork – observation
- using maps, atlases and globes – to locate cities, countries, continents and the 'Wonders of the World'

Geographical knowledge and understanding

- locational knowledge – Glasgow, world cities and wonders of the world
- place knowledge of the local area and world cities
- buildings and their functions
- iconic buildings around the world
- human features in urban areas – design, function and location of significant buildings; regeneration

To access extra resources from the Everyday Guides web page, see page 2.

©Ronnie Macdonald (Creative commons licence)

As the impressive *Riverside Museum* demonstrates, architecture is also an art form. The building is a development for the Glasgow Transport Museum at Pointhouse Quay in the Harbour regeneration district of Glasgow, Scotland. It was designed by the Iraqi-British architect Dame Zaha Mohammad Hadid (*b.* 1950). Hadid is famous for the 'powerful, curving forms of her elongated structures', and *Riverside* was voted European Museum of the Year in 2013. This dramatic piece of architecture is the ideal stimulus for investigating the design, function and location of iconic buildings. It can ignite pupil interest in discovering more about buildings that are seen as important locally, regionally, nationally and even internationally, and also encourage them to consider the part architecture plays in change and regeneration.

Sharing the architecture

Display a number of images of the *Riverside Museum* taken from different perspectives (see Everyday Guides webpage for links). What do the pupils think about this building? Do they like it? What do they think it is used for? Would they like to visit it? Elicit what the pupils know about architecture, and establish that all buildings, even seemingly insignificant ones, are designed by experts called architects.

Teaching activities

Art activity

Display images of different buildings (e.g. *Riverside Museum*, *The Shard* – see Everyday Guides webpage for links) as stimuli, invite pupils to design and build a model of their own special building. Provide construction kits as well as other materials. Some pupils will choose to work from experience to design a house or a school, while others will let their imagination go wild. Print photos of their completed models and ask pupils to annotate the images with information about the location, function and materials to be used for their building.

Our own special buildings

Explore the local area to identify any 'iconic' or special buildings. (If the school is located in a rural area, you may need to research buildings further afield.) Take photos and record any other information/observations. Why do people consider these buildings special or iconic? Which building is the most striking, impressive, historic, futuristic, tallest, biggest, and so on? What is the function of each one? Discuss whether the function has changed over time and how these changes may be apparent from the outside.

Back in school locate each building on a large-scale (1:1250 or 1:2500) OS map. Invite pupils to arrange the photos in different sequences, such as the order in which they saw the buildings, or the age or the function of the buildings. Use the photos to annotate the map with the location of each building.

To extend the fieldwork activity, pupils can create an 'iconic' or special buildings trail in the local area. Encourage them to include information, such as explanations of particular architectural features (doors, windows, roof lines), and an illustrated timeline showing historical changes in building styles and materials throughout the local area.

Buildings from different eras

Look at other examples of Hadid's work (see Everyday Guides webpage for links) and encourage the pupils to speculate on the function of each building. Discuss the materials used in the construction of modern buildings compared with buildings of the past. Invite the pupils to collect images of striking modern buildings from around the world. These can be used to create a display, which includes speech or thought bubbles around each image to encourage other pupils to add their responses to contemporary architecture.

Wonders of the world

To promote general geographical and specific locational knowledge, use the activity sheets that accompany this unit to encourage pupils to locate and mark on appropriate maps: 'The seven wonders of the ancient world', 'The seven wonders of the modern world' and 'The seven natural wonders of the world' (download the sheets from the Everyday Guides webpage). Ensure that pupils make full use of globes and atlases and record locations accurately. Invite pupils to design a poster or create a presentation on these iconic buildings and places and emphasise that they should justify the status of each as a 'wonder of the world'.

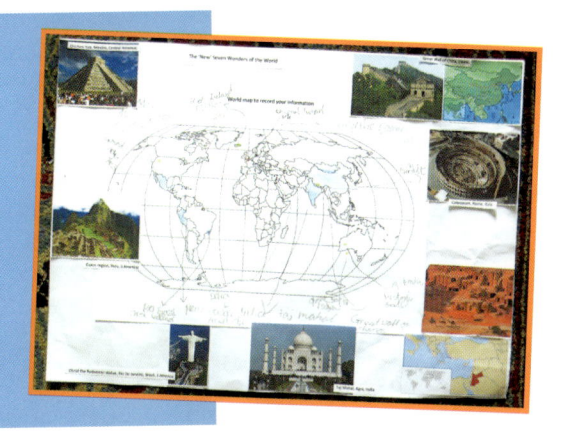

Future cities - regeneration or development?

The urban metropolis of Dubai (in the United Arab Emirates) and Shanghai (in China) are, perhaps, the most futuristic cityscapes on the planet. Dubai's iconic buildings include the Burj al Arab, the Burj Khalifa, the Rose Rayhaan by Rotana and Palm Jumeirah; while the Pudong skyline with the Shanghai Tower, the Shanghai World Financial Center [sic] and Jin Mao Tower contribute to Shanghai's unique skyline. Use images (sourced from the internet) of these futuristic cityscapes to inspire pupils to draw and map their own ideas for future cities.

©Sam Fifield

The Nenets of Northern Siberia

2008
photography by Sebastião Salgado

This black and white art photo is one of a series showing the harsh Polar environment of Northern Siberia, where the Nenet people live

Geographical enquiry and skills

- enquiry – asking and answering questions
- using geographical vocabulary
- using globes and world maps
- using the internet to research geographical information

Geographical knowledge and understanding

- locational knowledge – Polar regions
- place knowledge of Polar regions
- the significance of latitude for weather/climate patterns and vegetation
- physical geography of the Polar regions
- human geography of the Polar regions

To access extra resources from the Everyday Guides web page, see page 2.

This stunning black and white art photo is one of a series taken by Sebastião Salgado (b. 1944), a Brazilian photojournalist who lives in Paris and specialises in documenting people in their home and work environments. To capture The Nenets of Northern Siberia photos, Salgado lived with them for 40 days (see Everyday Guides webpage for more information). Salgado's images show just how much the Nenets rely on their reindeer for food, clothing, shelter and their livelihood. Salgado's series of photos of The Nenets of Northern Siberia can be used as the focus of an investigation of the Arctic – and Antarctic – regions: the places where the photos were taken, the weather and climate, the environment, and how people live in such extreme conditions.

Sharing the photographs

Display the photograph showing a Nenet woman in her sledge (see Everyday Guides webpage for links). Elicit pupil's first impressions. What do they think about this black and white photo? Would they prefer to see it in colour? Why? Show more of Salgado's photos, show different aspects of the lives of the Nenets, an indigenous nomadic people of Northern Siberia. Invite the pupils to describe the landscape, and to speculate about the place, the weather, the people and the type of animals that live there. If none of the pupils notice, point out that the large sledges are driven by women. What would it be like to be the woman in the picture? Why is she there? Where has the woman come from? Where might she be going? Discuss how the reindeer are adapted to the environment and weather in Northern Siberia.

Teaching activities

Art activity

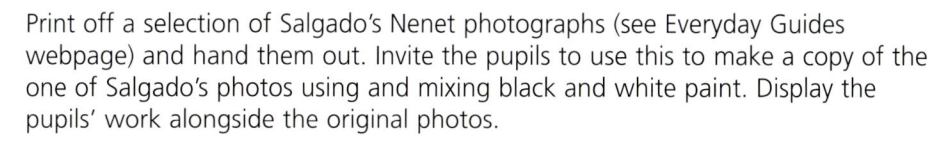

Print off a selection of Salgado's Nenet photographs (see Everyday Guides webpage) and hand them out. Invite the pupils to use this to make a copy of the one of Salgado's photos using and mixing black and white paint. Display the pupils' work alongside the original photos.

What is life like in very cold places?

First, pupils consider how we adapt our way of life to cope with the colder weather in winter. They may identify changes in clothing, food, the home, sports and pastimes, transport and daylight hours. Next, invite them to consider how they would live if it was extremely cold all year round. What would be the difficulties, challenges, advantages? Small groups of pupils could record their ideas, either on paper or using electronic notebooks (e.g. iPad), then compare their ideas.

Study Salgado's photographs to investigate the Nenets' way of life: pupils look for information about the Nenets' homes, clothes, food, transport and animals. Explain that the reindeer define the lives of the Nenets, providing food, clothing, shelter and transport (for example, reindeer meat is stored beneath the ice, Nenets make their coats and tents using reindeer hide). The Nenets are nomadic – spending winters near the Ob and Yenisey rivers and, when the weather warms up and becomes too hot for the reindeer, both animals and people head north into the Arctic Circle, where the reindeer can forage the tundra for vegetation. Ask pupils to compare their ideas about living in very cold climates with what they learn about the lives of the Nenets people (see Everyday Guides webpage for links).

Lines of latitude

Use a globe or wall map to locate Siberia where the photographs were taken. The photos provide a meaningful stimulus to teach about the North and South Pole, and lines of latitude and longitude – including the Arctic and Antarctic Circles, Tropics of Cancer and Capricorn and the Equator (download a base map from the Everyday Guides webpage).

Research the Polar regions

Use maps, books, and the internet to research the Arctic and Antarctic regions centred on the North and South Poles. As a class or in small groups, pupils study Pole-centric maps (download blank maps from the Everyday Guides webpage) and satellite images. Invite the pupils to identify their own questions about the Polar regions, these could include:

- How are the Polar regions similar to each other? How do they differ?
- What is the weather and climate like in each region? Just how cold do these parts of the world get? Is there summer and winter at the North and South poles?
- What animals and plants live in the Arctic and Antarctic? How are they are adapted to living in cold environments?
- What is under the snow and ice in the Arctic and the Antarctic?
- The continent at the South Pole is called Antarctica. Why is there not one called 'Arctica' at the North Pole?
- What effects does climate change have on the Polar regions?

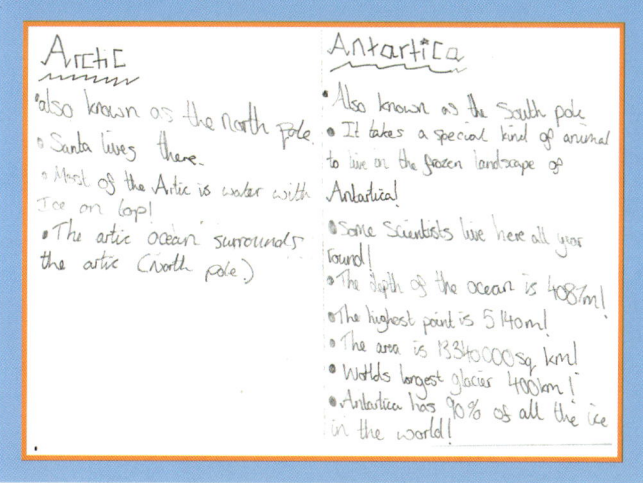

Use a globe to demonstrate the Earth's axial tilt of 23.5°. Use a torch to represent the sun's rays and demonstrate why the Poles experience 24 hours of daylight in their summer and 24 hours of darkness in their winter, and why it is cold throughout the year. Ask pupils to collect photos of the Polar regions and place each image around a North or South Pole-centric map (download blank maps from the Everyday Guides webpage).

175 The Almost Circle
1953
painted by Friedensreich Hundertwasser

© 2013 NAMIDA AG, Glarus, Switzerland. All rights reserved.

This oil painting represents a bird's eye view of the artist's experiences of journeys around Paris

Geographical enquiry and skills

- enquiry – asking and answering questions
- using geographical vocabulary
- identifying geographical features from aerial photographs
- using maps and atlases to locate world cities and continents.

Geographical knowledge and understanding

- locational knowledge – cities and continents around the world
- place knowledge of the local area and world cities
- road patterns in urban settlements
- land use in the local area
- spatial patterns in local and distant localities

To access extra resources from the Everyday Guides web page, see page 2.

Friedensreich Hundertwasser (1928–2000) was an Austrian architect, artist and environmentalist. His bold-coloured paintings, graphics, stamps, environmental posters and quirky architectural designs are a rich resource that pupils find exciting to work with. In his description of *175 The Almost Circle,* Hundertwasser revealed that he did not like straight lines. Along with many of Hundertwasser's works (see Everyday Guides webpage), this painting is an excellent starting point for exploring land use and transport networks, which can lead into investigating satellite images of local and distant places. It enables pupils to identify roads, railways and tracks, settlement patterns and other locational information, as well as exploring reasons for the journeys we and others make.

Sharing the painting

Display *175 The Almost Circle*, but, before revealing the title, ask pupils what they can see in the painting and invite them to think of a title for it. Discuss their titles and what the pupils 'see' in Hundertwasser's painting. Does it look like a map or aerial image, or is it something very different? What kind of area does it show: rural or urban? Explain that the painting represents journeys around Paris made by Friedensreich Hundertwasser. What do they notice about the routes? Friedensreich Hundertwasser's dislike of straight lines is apparent in this quote, 'Even if man is forced to walk through streets straight as a ruler, his personal, individual trail is never straight, but subject to his momentary impulses.' Reveal the title and use Hundertwasser's quote to encourage the pupils to share their non-linear journeys and diversions.

Teaching activities

Art activity

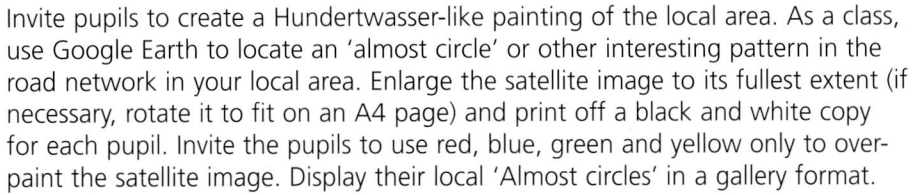

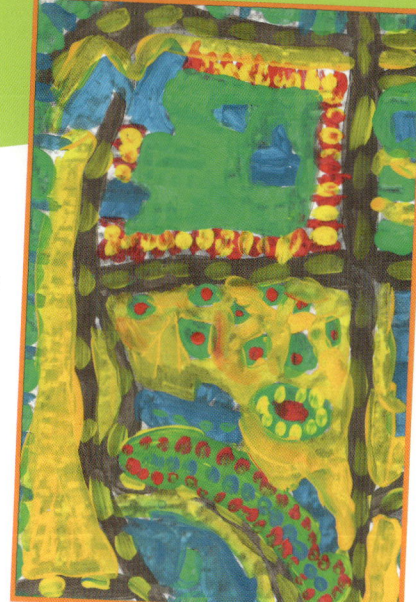

Invite pupils to create a Hundertwasser-like painting of the local area. As a class, use Google Earth to locate an 'almost circle' or other interesting pattern in the road network in your local area. Enlarge the satellite image to its fullest extent (if necessary, rotate it to fit on an A4 page) and print off a black and white copy for each pupil. Invite the pupils to use red, blue, green and yellow only to over-paint the satellite image. Display their local 'Almost circles' in a gallery format.

Exploring land use patterns

Display another of Friedensreich Hundertwasser's paintings – *241 City Seen from Beyond the Sun* (1955). What do the pupils think this painting shows? Could it be the street pattern of a city seen from a distance? (In discussions, one pupil observed 'You're either on top of the Eiffel Tower looking down, or beneath it looking up'.) Once pupils are told the title, *241 City...* readily conjures up streets enveloping a square city-centre piazza, park or lake, or the pupils may have other ideas.

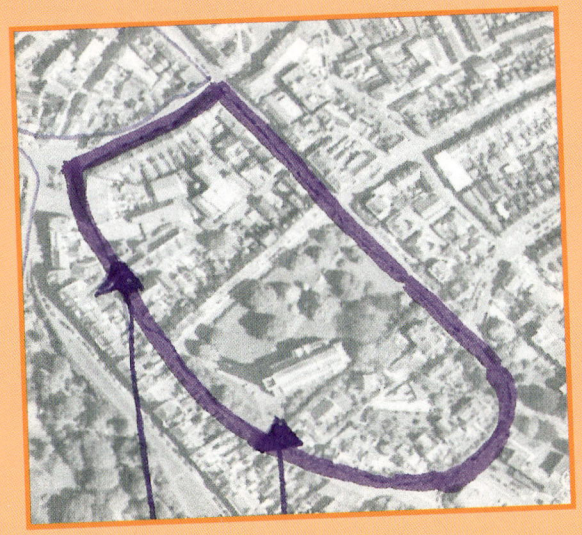

Use Google Earth to look at places the pupils are familiar within the local area, as well as other towns/cities if possible. Explore how land is used in urban settlements. Encourage pupils to identify and list areas of housing, the city centre, retail parks, industrial areas, municipal facilities (such as libraries and leisure centres), rivers, parks, and so on. Next, look at the textures and patterns of land use in rural areas identifying fields, woodlands, farms, villages, hills and valleys, lakes, reservoirs, rivers and streams. Again, list these features and/or label them.

Road patterns around the world

To strengthen pupils' global locational knowledge of major world cities, display both *175 The Almost Circle* and *241 City Seen from Beyond the Sun* and draw the pupils' attention to the concentric squares. Provide a list of cities from different continents and invite pupils to use maps and atlases to locate each city (download the 'Road patterns around the world' activity sheet from the Everyday Guides webpage).

Aerial views of our locality

Ask pupils to locate the school on Google Earth by entering the school post code. Use the zoom facility and Streetview, and encourage the pupils to identify different features in the local area, such as roads, buildings, gardens, parks, trees, water, fields, hedgerows, woodlands and, possibly, rivers, the coastline and the sea. As pupils discuss the images, facilitate the use of appropriate vocabulary to name features of the local area (see Everyday Guides webpage).

Having checked that they can recognise roads on the satellite image, pupils can then work in pairs. One pupil searches the area close to the school for a road pattern that interests them (the other pupil should not peek). The first pupil then describes this pattern to their partner; and the second pupil attempts to identify the roads – asking questions such as, is it north / south / east / west of the school? Are the roads straight, or curved? The pairs then swap over and the second pupil looks for an interesting road pattern. Pairs then share their road patterns with the rest of the class. How successful were the pupils at identifying their partner's road pattern? How did they locate it? Which questions were the most useful?

Red Slate Line
1986
created by Richard Long

This small-scale land art, which resembles a path, was displayed at the Yorkshire Sculpture Park near Wakefield in September 2012

Geographical enquiry and skills

- enquiry – asking and answering questions
- using geographical vocabulary
- fieldwork – observing and responding to landscape

Geographical knowledge and understanding

- features of the physical landscape
- the water cycle and the effects of water on rocks and landscape
- rocks and soils

To access extra resources from the Everyday Guides web page, see page 2.

Red Slate Line was created by the English sculptor, photographer and painter Richard Long CBE (*b.* 1946). He became associated with land art sculpture when the genre emerged in the 1960s and is now one of its best-known proponents. Most of Long's sculptures result from the epic walks he takes through remote areas of Britain and overseas. During fieldwork pupils can be inspired to create their own land art sculptures because, as Long says, such sculptures feed the senses at a place. Like Long, pupils can also take photographs and produce text work which feed the imagination *en plein air*. *Red Slate Line*, one of Long's smaller-scale sculptures, can stimulate pupils to think about land art, emotions and the concept of beauty in the rural landscape.

Sharing the sculpture

Show the pupils an image of *Red Slate* Line (see Everyday Guides webpage for links) and take the pupils through a guided visualisation or movement activity. Invite them to imagine themselves walking along a dark path through a wooded valley, ahead of them is a lake. What can they see, hear, feel? They come across *Red Slate Line* leading down towards the lake. How do they react? Do they want to walk along the *Line*? Why/why not? Next, explain that *Red Slate Line* is what is known as land art sculpture. What do they think of this kind of art? Does it enhance the place? What senses does it appeal to? Do they consider it art?

Teaching activities

Art activity

Look at some of Long's other land art sculptures – he has created a number of shapes in different settings (see Everyday Guides webpage for links). Explain that, in respecting nature Long does not make significant alterations to the landscapes: he either uses found materials – stone, wood and mud – to mark the ground, or rearranges the natural features of a place into basic geometric shapes (including spirals, circles, crosses and lines).

As land art sculptures are created outdoors, this activity is best carried out as fieldwork, but it can equally effectively be carried out in the classroom with an array of suitable materials. Select a suitable 'natural' location (moorland, beach, woodland, farmland, parkland or the school grounds) and ensure there is a supply of 'materials'. Encourage pupils to experiment with ideas and to take photos of their finished sculptures.

The emotional power of places

While Long believes that 'a sculpture feeds the senses at a place', places without sculptures also do the same. Encourage pupils to reflect on how different places and environments affect them. Which places make them feel happy, sad, calm, or anxious? Recall the human senses and ask pupils to suggest ways of measuring emotional reactions to different places. How could they measure their reaction to what they see, hear, smell and feel? Visit many and varied local environments (or use photographs in the classroom) and encourage the pupils to record, in a format of their choosing, how each place affects them. Discuss and analyse reactions.

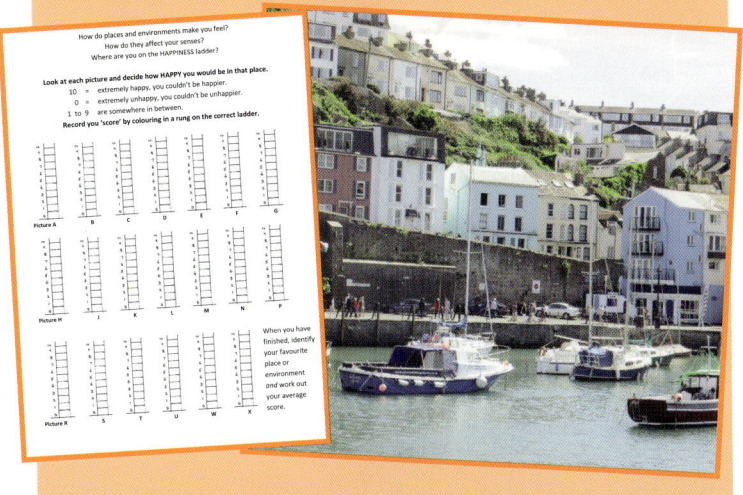

Investigating rocks

Richard Long says: 'I like the fact that every stone is different, one from another, in the same way all fingerprints, or snowflakes (or places) are unique, so no two circles can be alike'. Show pupils images of Long's stone-based land art to introduce aspects of physical geography.

Provide a selection of stones and pebbles and encourage pupils to sort them into different groups (by colour, textures, with/without fossils, with/without crystals) or sequence the stones (e.g. by size, weight, or colours). Provide magnifiers to enable pupils to study the rock samples carefully. They could use a simple rock identification guide to try to name the rocks and record their findings (download the 'Investigating rocks' sheet from the Everyday Guides webpage).

Water and rocks

Many of the stones Long uses for his work are sorted and rounded pebbles or boulders. Invite pupils to speculate how these stones got to be rounded. Visit a local stream or river to observe pebbles and boulders in situ on the river bed, embedded in the bank and deposited on the inside of meanders. Collect samples from different locations and compare them. Remind pupils about the water cycle. Investigate the role of rain, sea and river water in shaping rocks and landscape, including cliff and river erosion, rounding through rolling and angular fracturing by frost shattering.

Provide individual pupils with different rock samples and challenge them to produce a flow chart or story board that describes the history of 'their' rock.

21

Day and Night
1938
created by Maurits Cornelis Escher

This print from a woodcut shows day and night landscapes as mirror images

Geographical enquiry and skills

- enquiry – asking and answering questions
- use geographical vocabulary
- using globes, wall maps and atlases to locate the world's countries and major cities
- visual literacy – interpreting representations of landscape

Geographical knowledge and understanding

- locational knowledge – significant lines of longitude and latitude
- place knowledge of the local area and Dutch landscapes
- how the rotation of the earth produces day and night
- time zones and their impact on human activity
- physical and human features of selected locations

To access extra resources from the Everyday Guides web page, see page 2.

© 2014 The M.C. Escher Company – The Netherlands. All rights reserved.

Day and Night shows day-time and night-time versions of a landscape as mirror images. Pupils will find the fact that the white birds emerge from a daylight sky at the left, while the black birds blend into a night sky at the right, intriguing. Maurits Cornelis Escher (1898–1972) created *Day and Night* by carving mirror versions of the same design on two blocks of wood, coating the carved surfaces with ink then pressing the blocks onto paper. Escher, a Dutch graphic artist, produced mathematically-inspired woodcuts and lithographs, which often feature impossible constructions or explorations of infinity, architecture and tessellations. The print *Day and Night* can be used with pupils as a stimulus for investigating how the rotation of the Earth creates day and night, as well as learning about time zones.

Sharing the print

Display Esher's *Day and Night*. Can the pupils guess what the title of this print might be? What can they see in the image? Are there any clues as to the place the print is based on? With careful observation, pupils may spot the windmill(s) in the foreground and guess that it could be a Dutch landscape.

Teaching activities

Art activity

Study and discuss the pattern and colour used by Escher on the fields and birds to create the feeling of transformation between *Day and Night*. Relating to this tessellation in mathematics, invite the pupils to create their own work of art.

Pupils design a single image which they can use as a template to create a repeating pattern. Then ask them to select two colours and use shades of these two colours to depict a transformation in a landscape, e.g. between day and night, or autumn and winter.

Alternatively, take several photographs of a familiar location, e.g. the school playground or a local park, during the day and at night time. Ask the pupils to use collage techniques to create an image of their chosen location, with day on one side and night on the other. Show the pupils David Hockney's photo collages to give them an idea of the techniques involved (see Everyday Guides webpage for links). Ask the pupils to put themselves into their collage in the day and night sections. How do their feelings about this familiar location change? Discuss this, and how to keep ourselves safe in our local area.

Redesigning the mundane

Show pupils some of Escher's other works, for example *Relativity* (1953) and *Beledere* (1958) and *Waterfall* (1961) (see Everyday Guides webpage for links). Discuss whether Escher's structures would be possible in real life, or whether they are simply works of fantasy. Would the structures be practical? Does this matter? What is more important in architecture – function or style?

Invite pupils to consider the local landscape. What aspect of their everyday landscape would they change? What is the dullest aspect of the locality? Why? Can they redesign it without altering the function? Invite pupils to re-design the most mundane location in your local area, using construction materials, by drawing it freehand or using a computer (see Everyday Guides webpage for suggested packages). It may be possible to arrange to share these ideas within the local community, with local councillors or local authority planning officers.

Escher's landscape

Provide pairs of pupils with copies of *Day and Night*. Ask pupils first to identify and label the human and physical features in Escher's print then use Goggle Earth to locate images of Dutch landscapes which have the same features. Invite pupils to compare the Dutch landscape with Google Earth images of your local area, noting any features that are similar and any that are different (download the 'Comparing landscapes' sheet from the Everyday Guides webpage).

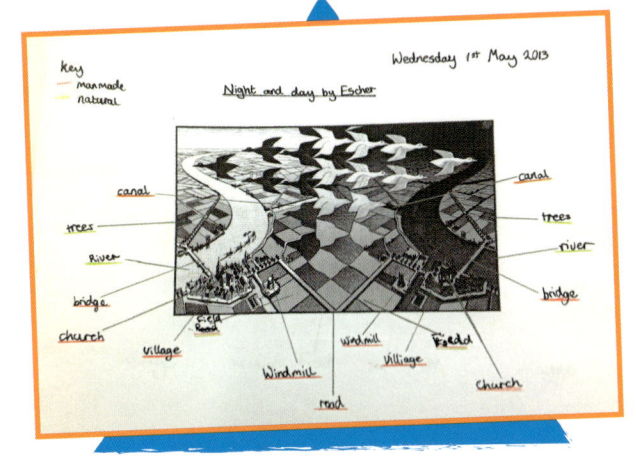

Investigating day and night

Using a globe and a torch, explain to the pupils why we have *day and night*. Locate lines of longitude and latitude on the globe and introduce the idea of time zones. As a class choose three locations in different time zones and find these places on the globe, on a wall map or in an atlas. Look at a webcam of each location. Discuss what time of day it is. Other than the level of sunlight, what clues are there? Encourage pupils to look at the activities of people, the amount of traffic, lights on inside buildings, and so on. (For websites and mobile apps to support this activity see Everyday Guides webpage.) Download the 'Children around the world' activity sheet (see Everyday Guides webpage) and ask the pupils to draw what they imagine pupils of the same age are doing in each of three locations at that exact moment. They add themselves in the fourth box.

Cattle Market, Braintree, Essex 1937
created by Edward Bawden

This lithograph from a linocut shows a livestock market in Braintree in England

Geographical enquiry and skills

- enquiry – asking and answering questions
- using geographical vocabulary
- using and making maps
- visual literacy

Geographical knowledge and understanding

- locational knowledge – countries importing foodstuff to the UK
- place knowledge of the local area
- human geography – trade in agricultural products, import and exports
- sustainable farming and fair trade
- the impact of human activity on climate change

To access extra resources from the Everyday Guides web page, see page 2.

Reproduced with permission © The Estate of Edward Bawden

This print shows a bustling area of cattle market in Braintree, a busy market town in Essex in 1937. Braintree cattle market functioned until the 1980s, when the market was closed down and replaced by a supermarket. Bawden's *Cattle Market, Braintree, Essex* can be used as a stimulus for investigating market places, the geography of food and local and international food trade patterns. The lithograph from a linocut, was created by Edward Bawden CBE (1903–1989) using a limited palette of colours. Bawden was an English painter, illustrator and graphic artist, most well-known for his prints, book covers, posters and garden metalwork furniture.

Sharing the print

First ask the pupils if they have ever been to a market. What was it like? What was on sale? Invite them to describe the experience using all their senses – they should draw on what they remember seeing, hearing, smelling, touching, tasting and feeling. Next, show the pupils Bawden's *Cattle Market, Braintree, Essex*. Have they ever seen animals on sale at a market? Invite pupils to put themselves into the scene and describe what they see, hear and smell, and add these as sticky notes to a print-out of the lithograph with their comments.

Teaching activities

Art activity

Visit a local market or greengrocer's and ask pupils to sketch three products of their choosing. Back at school invite each pupil to choose a small section or a motif from their sketch, from which to create a print. Ask the pupils to copy their chosen design onto a polystyrene tile using a pencil to create indentations of it the motif in the tile. After spreading paint or ink evenly over the tile with a roller, they then turn the tile over and press it down firmly on a sheet of paper. Pupils can work in groups to create repeating patterns that depict the products that are available locally. Create a display that emulates the market stalls or a greengrocer's display.

Our local market

Visit a local market or greengrocer's to look at the variety of fresh produce. With the proprietor's permission, pupils take photographs of the fresh fruit and vegetables and record which ones were produced locally, which were produced elsewhere in the UK, and which have been imported. Back at school, link each item's photo to its country of origin on a world map. Pupils could create individual maps, or work towards a whole-class foodstuffs display.

Investigate how products get to the market and introduce the concepts of trade, imports and exports. Ask pupils to think about the advantages and disadvantages of international trade in fruit and vegetables. What would not be on sale in the local market/greengrocer's if there was no international trade? What would the impact be on their diet? What impact would there be on people's work in the UK and abroad? Pupils can record their ideas and comments on the 'Local and imported food' activity sheet (download from the Everyday Guides webpage) and use these to inform a piece of writing in the discussion genre.

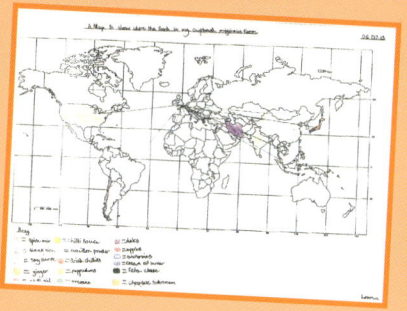

Food miles

Buy a selection of packed-lunch items from the local supermarket and ask pupils to plan a lunch that they would like to eat using the products. After each pupil has selected their ingredients, they should look at the packets for information on where each item was grown or produced. Invite them to use an atlas to locate the countries and then create a 'meal map' on an outline map. Next, pupils use an online food miles calculator to calculate the total distance travelled by the meal (see Everyday Guides webpage for food-mile calculator links).

Explain that food transport is responsible for the UK adding nearly 19 million tonnes of carbon dioxide to the atmosphere each year. Challenge pairs of pupils to think of a meal with the fewest possible food miles. Which pair can produce the best meal idea? Encourage them to use an online food miles calculator to test their ideas and refine their thinking.

Investigate fair trade

Introduce or revisit the concept of fair trade. Fair trade is about attaining better prices, decent working conditions, local sustainability and fair terms of trade for farmers and workers in the developing world. Ask pupils, working in small groups, to research the concept of fair trade (see Everyday Guides webpage for links). What does it mean? How can consumers recognise fairly traded products? Pupils may spot the FAIRTRADE Mark which is licensed by the Fairtrade Foundation for use on products that meet international Fairtrade standards. What fair trade products are available locally? Is fair trade an initiative the school could or should support? Do they feel they should do something, and if so, what? Pupils can report their findings on fair trade through a presentation, video or audio report for the school website.

Sustainable shopping app

Following their work, pupils could create an App on either food miles or fair trade for a smartphone or notepad. Their App's aim is to offer shoppers advice on how to make more sustainable and fairly-traded product choices in their day-to-day purchases. As well as information on the principles behind fair trade, pupils could include advice on which foods to buy from local shops/supermarkets and each outlet's fair trade policy. The Everyday Guides webpage includes links to appropriate App-building packages.

Paintings of London and Venice
by Canaletto and Monet

This oil painting depicts a view of St Pauls Cathedral and the Thames in London in the eighteenth century

© The Lobkowicz Collections, Prague Castle, Czech Republic

Geographical enquiry and skills

- enquiry – asking and answering questions
- using geographical vocabulary
- using maps and atlases to locate UK and global cities and countries
- using aerial photographs and mapping at different scales

Geographical knowledge and understanding

- locational knowledge – towns and cities in the UK and wider world
- place knowledge of London and Venice
- why settlements develop on river crossing points

To access extra resources from the Everyday Guides web page, see page 2.

This unit demonstrates how famous historical paintings of London (Canaletto's *The River Thames with St Paul's Cathedral on Lord Mayor's Day* (c. 1746) and Monet's *The Thames below Westminster* (1871)) and Venice (*A Regatta on the Grand Canal* (1735) by Canaletto and *The Church of San Giorgio Maggiore, Venice* (1908) by Monet) can be used as a stimulus for investigating urban settlements. The landscape painter Giovanni Antonio Canal (1697–1768) was born in Venice. Better known as Canaletto, he painted grand scenes of the city's pageantry and traditions. Canaletto moved to London in 1746 and immediately began producing views of the city. Claude Monet (1840–1926) was a founder of French impressionist painting. Monet believed in expressing one's perceptions of nature, especially through *plein-air* landscape painting. Like Canaletto, Monet moved to London in 1870–1. In 1908, Monet spent three months in Venice.

Sharing the paintings

Display both Canaletto's *The River Thames with St. Paul's Cathedral on Lord Mayor's Day* and Monet's *The Thames below Westminster* (see Everyday Guides webpage for links), and ask pupils if they know the place shown in the paintings. What features do they recognise? What are the similarities and differences between the two paintings? Compare these scenes with Canaletto and Monet's paintings of Venice. Can pupils identify which painting was produced by each artist? Which style of painting do they prefer? Why? Explain that the two styles represent different ways of perceiving and representing urban landscapes.

Teaching activities

Art Activity

Before venturing outside, discuss and compare Canaletto's accurate, topographical style of painting with Monet's looser impressionism. Monet, interested in the emotion or impression of a place rather than accuracy of portrayal, applied unblended colours with brushstrokes that barely convey forms, but that emphasise the effects of light. Canaletto tended to paint scenes in a 'postcard' or photographic style.

Either in the school grounds or the local area, ask pupils to create their own painting. They should use either Canaletto's or Monet's style and focus either on accuracy or on creating an 'impression' of the scene. Afterwards, invite pupils to write a caption that can be hung alongside their artwork (as is standard practice in art galleries); it must explain their artistic choices.

Locating landmarks on maps

Discuss how pupils might find the locations of Canaletto and Monet's paintings on a map. Establish that first they need to find the country, then the city, then the particular area of the city depicted in the paintings. Use Google Earth and/or Google maps to zoom in, switch to Street view to see a present-day view of London and Venice. What landmarks can they identify? Pupils compare the historical paintings with the modern satellite images, looking for similarities and differences.

Demonstrate how to locate buildings on a map. Iconic buildings such as Big Ben have a distinctive shape in the oblique view of a painting, but its plan shape appears unremarkable on a map. Make a list of landmark buildings in London (e.g. Buckingham Palace, Houses of Parliament, Tower of London, the London Eye) and in Venice (e.g. the Rialto Bridge, the Grand Canal, St Michael's Basilica) and challenge pupils to find each one using Google Earth. Encourage them to zoom in to explore the environment around each building/landmark.

Picture postcards

Canaletto painted accurate views of Venice for wealthy visitors, often on a 'Grand tour' of Europe, to buy as mementos of their time in the city. Today we might take a photograph or buy a postcard to send to our friends and family at home.

Collect postcards of the local area. Discuss why these views have been chosen. What types of locations / landmarks are depicted? Do they include old or significant buildings, local beauty spots, scenic views, busy streets, open spaces? What image of the local area do they portray? Invite pupils to choose a view of their own locality for a postcard. Why this particular view? They could photograph or draw their view, print it out and mount it on a postcard. If possible, after pupils have written a message on the reverse (which includes details about the locality), arrange a postcard exchange with another school (see Everyday Guides for ideas).

Rivers and canals in cities

Use Canaletto and Monet's paintings of London and Venice as the focus of a discussion on the difference between rivers and canals. Locate and follow waterways on maps of the two cities. Can pupils explain why people have always settled by waterways? Why do people tend to construct settlements at river crossing points? Why have canals been built? What purpose do they serve?

To develop their locational knowledge of the UK, invite pupils to record places in the UK that include the name of a river (e.g. Newcastle Upon Tyne, Burton on Trent) on the 'UK cities and rivers' activity sheet (download it from the Everyday Guides webpage). They should use atlases and maps to trace the course of each named river, and say whether it flows into other rivers or directly to the sea (for example, Burton on Trent is located in the Midlands; from Burton the River Trent flows north-eastwards and feeds into the River Humber which flows into the North Sea).

Surprised! (or Tiger in a Tropical Storm)
1891
painted by Henri Rousseau

This oil painting depicts a tiger in an imaginary tropical rainforest environment

Geographical enquiry and skills

- enquiry – asking and answering questions
- using geographical vocabulary
- using primary and secondary resources to investigate rainforests
- using globes, maps and atlases

Geographical knowledge and understanding

- locational knowledge – global location of tropical rainforests
- climate zones, biomes and vegetation belts
- the features of rainforests – plants, animals, weather and climate
- local/global links
- the impact of human activity in rainforests on climate change

To access extra resources from the Everyday Guides web page, see page 2.

Reproduced with permission © National Gallery, London, England

Surprised! was the first of the jungle scenes that Henri Rousseau (1844–1910) became famous for painting. Rousseau described the painting as representing a tiger hunting explorers – so it became known as *Tiger in a Tropical Storm (Surprised!)*. Rousseau taught himself to paint and, although his style was ridiculed during his lifetime, since the artist died his talent has been recognised. His simplistic style is now copied by other artists: pupils may have encountered Rousseau-like paintings in children's picture books. *Tiger in a Tropical Storm* provides an ideal starting point for an investigation of rainforests and the plants and animals that live in them. It also lends itself to encouraging pupils to consider the value and reliability of paintings as a source of information about places.

Sharing the painting

Invite the pupils to look carefully at Rousseau's *Tiger in a Tropical Storm*. What sort of environment do they think it depicts? What kind of clues are there in the painting? Discuss the plants and animal. What do these suggest about the weather and climate? Establish that the painting shows a tropical rainforest by drawing pupils' attention to salient features (including the dense, lush undergrowth and the thick canopy of trees). Although Rousseau claimed knowledge of the jungle while in Mexico, it is more likely that he drew inspiration from visits to Parisian hothouses and zoos. Do pupils think *Tiger in a Tropical Storm* is a realistic representation of a rainforest? Why/why not? Discuss whether the accurate depiction of reality is important in art.

Teaching activities

Art activity

Work together as a class to research, design and create a large rainforest frieze or convert a corridor into a rainforest. It should illustrate all the features of a rainforest environment. Challenge pupils to demonstrate all they learn about rainforest environments, the plants and animals as well as the weather and climate, though this artwork.

Investigating rainforests

Ask pairs of pupils to talk about what we can learn about the rainforest from *Tiger in a Tropical Storm*. Sort their answers into categories (e.g. weather and climate, landscape, plants, animals) then give each pair a photograph of the rainforest and ask them to repeat the same activity (download the 'Using paintings and photographs' activity sheet from the Everyday Guides webpage). Provide extra photos in order to demonstrate the value of studying additional images.

Introduce, or revise, the concept of primary and secondary sources with pupils. Discuss the similarities and differences between the photos (a primary source) and Rousseau's painting (a secondary source). Which provides more accurate information about the rainforest? Finally, discuss whether accuracy is important when you are trying to answer geographical questions.

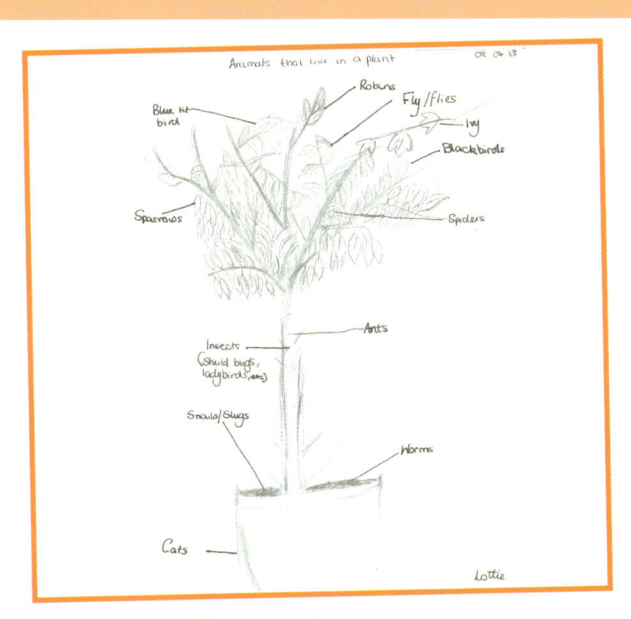

Why rainforests matter

Using a number of secondary sources, investigate how the rainforests affect our lives in the UK and why they matter. Introduce pupils to the concept of biodiversity, describe some of the huge variety of plants and animals that live in and rely on the world's rainforests.

Challenge pupils to find out why rainforests matter. Working in small groups, they could look at rainforests as a source of food and medicine, a habitat for plants and animals, as climate regulators, and/or rainforests as a home for people. Following the research, each group then presents their findings as a news report or documentary to the class in a format (e.g. video, audio, slide presentation) of their choosing.

Locating rainforests

Use an environmental globe or atlas to identify where tropical rainforests are located. Can pupils see a pattern in the location of rainforests? Encourage them to look at the distribution of rainforest in relation to the Equator and the Tropics. Are there rainforests in every continent? Discuss why this is the case.

Use Google Earth to find images of different rainforests. Invite small groups or individual pupils to choose a particular rainforest or area of rainforest for a case study. Challenge them to locate where that rainforest is and find out what type of rainforest it is (including mangrove, lowland, cloud and temperate) and what this label means. Pupils can also investigate the climate, the plants and animals that are found in their rainforest. Explain that each group/individual must produce a poster for a class display. The posters can be positioned around a world map to indicate the distribution of the different types of rainforests.

Biodiversity in the local area

Identify a mature tree in the local area and take the pupils to study it. They should look for evidence of the variety of organisms that rely on the tree. Invite pupils to draw the tree and the plants, birds, animals, insects, etc., they observe in and around the tree (e.g. tree creeper, squirrel, woodpecker, ants, butterflies, primroses). Discuss the different habitats within the tree. Which parts of the tree do the animals / birds / insects inhabit? Which animals use all of the tree, and which ones use part of it? This discussion provides an opportunity to introduce the concept of rainforest layers: forest floor, undergrowth, canopy and emergent layer.

Record the fieldwork by taking photos and create a montage, invite pupils to annotate it with captions or sticky notes recording what they have learned.

Cotopaxi, Ecuador
1989
painted by the Quechuan people

Source: with permission from the volcanism blog
http://volcanism.wordpress.com/category/saturday-volcano-art

This painting shows the Andean landscape in Ecuador, with the volcano, Cotopaxi, clearly visible in the background

Geographical enquiry and skills

- enquiry – asking and answering questions
- using geographical vocabulary
- visual literacy
- using maps, globes, satellite images and indigenous art
- extracting information from a digital interactive map

Geographical knowledge and understanding

- locational knowledge – South America, Ecuador, Quito
- location of major mountainous and volcanic regions of the world
- place knowledge of Ecuador, South America
- physical geography – volcanoes and earthquakes
- human geography – life in Tigua, an Ecuadorian mountain village

To access extra resources from the Everyday Guides web page, see page 2.

The *Cotopaxi, Ecuador* painting is one of many produced by Quechuan people living in Tigua, a village situated high in the Central Andes and south-west of the capital of Ecuador, Quito. This painting records village life for the Quechuan people in the beautiful Andean mountain landscape, with the snow-capped Cotopaxi visible in the distance (at 5897m Cotopaxi is the world's highest active volcano). Like most traditional Tiguan artworks, *Cotopaxi, Ecuador* is painted on sheepskin. As pupils often find the bright colours and subject matter of *Cotopaxi, Ecuador* appealing, using the painting as a stimulus is a great way to immerse them in an investigation of volcanoes, as well as looking at life in a village in Ecuador, South America.

Sharing the painting

As you look at *Cotopaxi, Ecuador* discuss the landscape, the Quechuan people, their lives and their animals. Encourage pupils to speculate about what it would be like to live here. What interests the pupils most about the painting? Explain that the scene has been painted on sheepskin. Why do pupils think this is used? Next, provide an alternative view of the volcano by displaying Frederic Edwin Church's *Cotopaxi* (1855). Encourage pupils to compare the two paintings. After they have identified the similarities ask pupils to describe any differences. Which differences do they think are due to changes over time? Which are due to the artists' choosing what to portray about the area? And which attributed to what the artists' believed viewers would be most interested in?

Teaching activities

Art activity

Invite pupils to design and create a colourful picture in the style of the Tiguan painting, showing their own way of life and local landscape, that tourists might be interested in buying. Before starting the task discuss what pupils think is special about their local area. Which elements do they think are the most important and should be included, in terms of the landscape, the buildings, the people, their activities (e.g. festivals) and so on?

Where is Cotopaxi (and Vesuvius)?

Display another of Frederic Edwin Church's *Cotopaxi* (1861) paintings together with Joseph Mallard William Turner's *Vesuvius in Eruption* (1820), both of which show volcanic eruptions. Pupils are probably more accustomed to viewing films of (or visualising) volcanoes erupting – with red-hot lava pouring down the hillside and/or volcanic ash being thrown high into the sky. Invite pupils to imagine viewing the scene in each painting from Church and Turner's standpoint. What would it be like to witness a volcanic eruption? How might an erupting volcano sound? What do they think it would smell like? How would the eruption feel underfoot?

Locating volcanoes

Cotopaxi, one of the few Equatorial volcanoes in the world, lies approximately 27km south of Quito – the capital of Ecuador. The volcano is situated in the Andes, the longest continental mountain chain in the world (7000km in extent) – stretching through Argentina, Bolivia, Chile, Colombia, Ecuador, Peru and Venezuela. Use physical and political globes, atlases and satellite images to locate the Andes in South America as well as Ecuador, Quito, Tigua, and Cotopaxi.

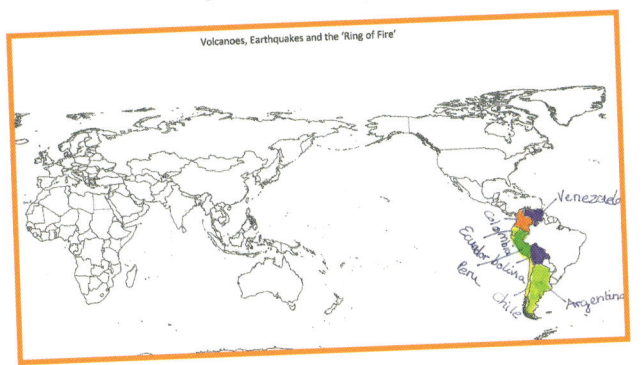

Next, challenge pupils to identify other active volcanoes in South America then extend the study to volcanoes in the rest of the world. Invite pupils to use online sources to discover more about active (and dormant) volcanoes. Challenge pupils to create a 3D map to show the location of the world's major mountain ranges and volcanoes (see Everyday Guides webpage for links).

Volcanoes and tectonic plates

Use the animated map created by Volcano Discovery (see Everyday Guides webpage for link) to encourage pupils to look for any patterns in the global distribution of volcanoes. They should be able to identify two curve-shaped clusters: one down the west coast of South America and the other from Japan to New Zealand. Encourage them to recognise that both lie around the Pacific Ocean and introduce or revisit the correct vocabulary, by using such terms as 'plate tectonics' and 'Pacific Ring of Fire'.

Display and discuss an online map of tectonic plates (see Everyday Guides webpage for link). Challenge pupils to compare the active volcanoes and plate tectonics maps. What do they notice about the locations of Cotopaxi and Vesuvius in relation to the plate boundaries? How could these volcanoes have formed? Encourage pupils to find out more about what happens at plate boundaries, where lava comes from and how and why volcanoes erupt.

What is life like in Tigua?

Print a number of different Tiguan artworks and challenge pairs of pupils to find out about Andean life and landscape as the Tiguan people represent it. Pupils should be able to describe Tiguans feeding their sheep and llamas, spinning wool, weaving cloth, and harvesting potatoes, barley and maize. Invite the pairs of pupils to annotate different images, looking for clues about the physical and human geography of the area. Can they identify specific aspects of life (e.g. a medicine man, feasts or festivals)? Do they think Andean life is really like this?

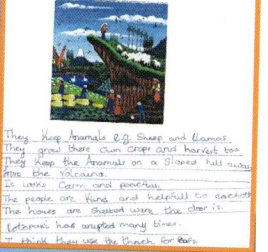

Challenge the pupils to discover what the Andean landscape and life there is really like? They should locate Cotopaxi and Tigua on satellite images and zoom in and out comparing the information obtained from the Tiguan paintings with the satellite images (download the 'Comparing paintings and satellite images' activity sheet from the Everyday Guides webpage).

London Underground Map 1933
created by Harry Beck

This topological map shows the London Underground system in 1933 as a series of coloured lines

Geographical enquiry and skills

- enquiry – asking and answering questions, collecting data
- using geographical vocabulary, especially related to maps
- using and making maps

Geographical knowledge and understanding

- locational knowledge – London and its region
- place knowledge of London and its region
- London's transport systems
- different types of maps

To access extra resources from the Everyday Guides web page, see page 2.

Reproduced with permission © London Transport Museum

In the 1930s, Henry (Harry) Beck (1902–1974) worked as an engineering draftsman at the London Underground Signals Office. The Underground was expanding rapidly, so it was increasingly difficult to communicate route information accurately, especially when the lines were superimposed onto a London road map. Beck thought that passengers were more interested in how to get from one Tube station to another and where to change trains than they were in the map's geographical accuracy, so he chose to base his design for the Underground map on electrical circuit diagrams. In doing so, Beck created the *London Underground Map* (see Everyday Guides webpage for more on his approach), which is ideal for stimulating an investigation of maps as art and a means to communicate spatial information. It can also be used to promote pupils' knowledge of London (including its landmarks) and to encourage them to develop map-reading and route-finding skills.

Sharing the map

Display Beck's *London Underground Map* and establish whether any pupils recognise it. What is familiar about the map? Encourage them to point out the names of places they know. Explain that this map of the London Underground system was drawn up more than 80 years ago. Do pupils think it could be used today? Why/why not? They may be surprised to discover that, in 1933 almost all of the Tube lines were north of the River Thames.

Teaching activities

Art activity

With help from the pupils and other adults, gather a range of maps, including pictorial atlases and globes and discuss them as examples of cartographers' artistry. Invite the pupils to choose one map and find out more about its design. (For example, in describing his approach to the 1933 *London Underground Map*, Harry Beck said he thought 'it might be possible to tidy up [the old map] by straightening the lines, experimenting with diagonals and evening out the distance between stations'.) Pupils may comment that some maps are beautiful, but can they identify what makes a good map design? Is it form, function, aesthetics, simplicity, or a combination of these things? Which maps do the pupils like best and why?

Invite pupils to create a map of a place they are very familiar with, such as the school grounds, a local street or their favourite park. Encourage the pupils to draw their map in the same style as their favourite map.

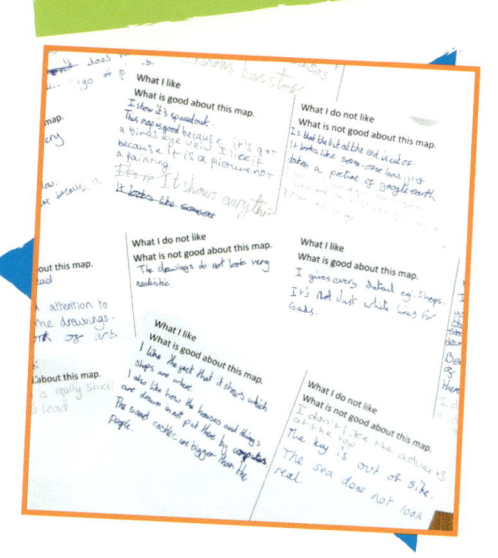

The modern tube map

Provide pupils with copies of the present-day London Underground map and invite them to compare it with Beck's 1933 map. If they do not mention it, point out that, although the Tube network has expanded considerably, present-day London Underground maps continue to be based on Beck's schematic design. Which areas of London have changed the most? Can they find out why there were very few Tube lines south of the River Thames in the 1930s? What does this indicate? Encourage pupils to provide explanations for their observations.

Working either in small groups or in pairs, pupils use the modern London Underground maps (including the key) to set challenges for each other. For example, 'You live in Edgware. How would you get to the Natural History Museum in South Kensington? Where would you change trains?' The pupils must identify different start points and include landmarks to be visited along the route, such as the Tower of London or the London Eye.

Geographical or topological maps?

You will need a copy of the Transport for London Underground (topological) and Central London bus (geographical) maps for each group of pupils (see Everyday Guides webpage for links). First, each group should focus on a different Underground line. The groups follow and then transfer the route and stations from their Underground line onto the bus map, using felt pen. Next, they should compare the line on each of the two maps. What do they notice? What are the advantages and disadvantages of each map? Encourage the groups to list the pros and cons of travelling by bus and by Tube in London. Discuss whether one method of transport is better than the other, and what we mean by 'better' – fastest, easiest, most scenic, or another reason.

Mapping our journeys

Discuss and list all the journeys in and around school that the class makes – to assembly, to a particular room (ICT suite?), to PE or games. Record these journeys on a large plan of the school, using a different colour for each one. Challenge small groups of pupils to simplify the resulting geographical map (one that is spatially accurate because it has been drawn onto a plan of the school) and make it into a topological map like Beck's *London Underground Map* (one with straight lines and points for locations/features). Explain that they must decide whether to include a key for the journey taken, a scale and/or a North pointer, and what labels to include on the maps.

Once they have completed this activity, pupils could create a personal journey map centred on their home area (this could be done over a given period – one or two weeks). Where possible provide large-scale base maps. Explain that the pupils should use different colours for each place visited; the types of transport used; and for journeys made on different days. If pupils elect to carry out the mapping activity over one or two weeks, encourage them to look for any patterns that emerge. What is their favourite journey and why? Which places do they visit most/least?

Northumberlandia, the Lady of the North
2010
created by Charles Jencks

This enormous land-sculpture of a reclining lady lies in the Cheviot Hills in Northumberland National Park

Geographical enquiry and skills
- enquiry – asking and answering questions
- using geographical vocabulary
- using photographs and satellite images
- using maps and atlases
- fieldwork – observing and recording geographical features

Geographical knowledge and understanding
- location of Northumberland, and National Parks in the UK
- physical geography of landscapes
- human geography – mining and quarrying
- environmental issues associated with primary industry
- development and designation of community and National Parks
- tourism in National Parks locations

To access extra resources from the Everyday Guides web page, see page 2.

© Graeme Peacock

The construction of *Northumberlandia, the Lady of the North*, a spectacular example of landscape art (or land-sculpture) near Cramlington in the Northumberland National Park, began in 2010. Designed by the landscape architect, Charles Jencks (*b.* 1939), its name comes from the sculpture's form: a 0.4km-long reclining lady. *Northumberlandia* was constructed adjacent to Shotton open-cast coal mine on a greenfield site donated by the Blagdon Estate. Like many of Jencks' sculptural landscapes, *Northumberlandia* features grassy spiral mounds – these were constructed from waste from the mine. The sculpture includes 6km of public footpaths, enabling visitors to view the mine from the top. *Northumberlandia* can be used as the stimulus for investigating public art, community and National Parks, quarrying, mining and land restoration.

Sharing Jencks' land-sculpture

Display an image of *Northumberlandia, the Lady of the North* (see Everyday Guides webpage) and ask pupils what they think it is. How big do they think it is? Invite the pupils to study aerial images and photographs of the site and surrounding landscape, especially ones that include people so they get some idea of the scale of the sculpture. Establish whether any pupils know where the sculpture is. What does the sculpture represent? What do they think it is made of? How do they think it is used? How do they feel about the sculpture? Do they think it is beautiful or ugly?

Teaching activities

Art activity

Provide modelling materials, such as wet sand or clay and encourage the children to create a model of a reclining figure in the style of *Northumberlandia, the Lady of the North*, or to devise an alternative design for a land-sculpture that is suitable for a local park.

Can land-sculptures make landscapes more beautiful?

Explain that *Northumberlandia* is an unusual land-sculpture: its construction was focused on the use of waste material from the adjacent open-cast mine. Rather than follow the usual practice of returning the waste material to the mine and landscaping the area, some 1.5 million tonnes of excavated rock was incorporated into the sculpture. It cost £3 million to create *Northumberlandia*, just to provide a landscape for the local community to enjoy. Do pupils think it was money well spent?

Look at, discuss and evaluate other examples of Charles Jenck's work. Elicit pupils' opinions of sculptures of different scales that are placed in the landscape, such as Antony Gormley's *Angel of the North* (1998) near Gateshead, and Barbara Hepworth's artworks in her garden at Tate St Ives in Cornwall (see Everyday Guides webpage for links). Do the pupils think these works of art enhance or detract from the landscape in which they are set? Would the landscape be more beautiful without them?

Scars on the landscape?

Discuss the presence of mining and quarrying in the landscape. As primary industries, both involve extraction of the Earth's resources (such as coal, clay, rock, sand, gravel, or minerals), so mines can only be sited where these resources are located. Draw pupils' attention to the fact that in the UK the extractive industries were much more active than they are today, but that evidence of these activities is widespread and found in most areas.

Locate a quarry or mine in or near the local area as the focus for the pupils' work. (Sites that are no longer being worked can be just as interesting as those that are currently active.) Visit the site and, observing all health and safety precautions, allow pupils to investigate it for themselves. Where is it? What resource has been extracted? How (by what process) has it been acquired? How has the quarry/mine marked the landscape? Has the landscape been restored in any way? What is the result – has the landscape been improved, or ruined, or something in between? Invite pupils to use the information they collect to create case study materials on the mine or quarry either for other year groups within your school, or (if you have one) pupils in your twinned school.

Our National Parks

Introduce (or revisit) the idea of National Parks and Areas of Outstanding Natural Beauty (AONBs), explaining that because human activity can destroy a landscape, where an area of countryside is perceived as a valuable resource, nowadays it tends to be protected by law. In the UK and other countries, this includes National Parks and AONBs. Provide the class with a list of National Parks in the UK (see Everyday Guides webpage for links). Challenge small groups of pupils to locate different Parks on a map of the UK and discover what is special about each one in terms of landscape and wildlife. Do they think that people simply appreciate the beauty of the landscape, or the presence of water, high ground or wildness? Or is it something else? Would it be possible to 'measure' landscape beauty?

Arrange a visit to the nearest National Park or an AONB, so that pupils can experience the special qualities of the landscape at first-hand through sensory fieldwork and other activities.

Useful resources

Barbe-Gall, F. (2005) *How to Talk to Children about Art*. London: Frances Lincoln.

Barlow, C. and Brook, A (2009) 'Valuing my place: how can collaborative work between geography and art make the usual bcome unusual?' in Rowley, C. and Cooper, H. (eds) *Cross Curricular Approaches Towards Teaching and Learning*. London: Sage, pp. 49–74.

Barlow, C. and Brook, A. (2010) '*Geography and art: local area work*', *Primary Geographer*, 72, pp. 16–17.

Barnes, R. (2002) *Teaching Art to Young Children*. London/New York: Routledge/Falmer.

Bowden, J. with Ogier, S. and Gregory, P. (2013) *Art and Design Primary Coordinator's Handbook*. Glasgow: Belair/NSEAD.

Deas, S., Meager, N., Bruce, R., Springett-McHugh, N., Van Rhyn, C., Julie Ashfield, J., Springett-McHugh, S., and Newbury P. (2013) *Projects Inspired by Neighbourhoods – Belair on Display* London: Collins Educational.

Fabian, Meg (2005) *Drawing is a Class Act: A Skills-based Approach to Drawing*, Brilliant Publications.

Fabian, Meg (2010) Painting – *A Skills-based Approach*, Brilliant Productions.

Horler, T. with Mackintosh, M., Kavanagh, P. and Kent, G. (2014) 'The art of perceiving landscapes', *Primary Geography*, 83, pp. 8–10.

Kohl and Solga (2008) *Discovering Great Artists: Hands-On Art for Children in the Styles of the Great Masters*, Bright Ring Publishing, U.S.

Mackintosh, M. (2013) 'Representing places in maps and art' in Scoffham, S. (ed) *Teaching Geography Creatively*. Abingdon/New York: Routledge, pp. 74–84.

Martin and Owens (2008) *Caring for Our World: A Practical Guide to ESD for Ages 4–8*, Sheffield: Geographical Association.

Meager, N. (2011) Creativity and Culture: Art projects for primary schools. Glasgow: NSEAD.

Meager, N. (2012) *Teaching Art 7–11*. Glasgow: Belair/NSEAD.

Scoffham, S. (ed) (2010) *Primary Geography Handbook* (revised edition). Sheffield: Geographical Association.

Scoffham, S. (ed) (2013) *Teaching Geography Creatively*. Abingdon/New York: Routledge.

Stephens, K. (1994) *Learning Through Art and Artefacts*, Hodder Education.

Tanner, J. (2013) 'Geography and the creative arts' in Scoffham, S. (ed) *Teaching Geography Creatively*. Abingdon/New York: Routledge, pp. 128–42.

Tanner, J. and Whittle, J. (2013) *Everyday Guide to Primary Geography: Story*, Sheffield: Geographical Association.

Tinker, C. (2011) *Hands on Geography*. Glasgow: Belair.

Williams, D (1999) *Step by Step: Art,* Preston: Topical Resources

Williams, D (2005) *Step by Step: Art in the Geography Lesson*, Preston: Topical Resources.

Witt, S. (2010) 'Geography and art: happy spaces, happy places', *Primary Geographer,* 72, pp. 18–19.

Witt, S. and Sudbury, J. (2010) 'Geography and art: a sense of place at Bishop's Waltham Junior School', *Primary Geographer*, 72, pp. 20–21.

Relevant materials on the GA website

Mackintosh, M. (2003) 'The art of geography' available at www.geography.org.uk/download/GA_EYPMackintoshPG03.pdf

Primary Geography (2010), 72, for articles focusing on Geography and Art.

Primary Geography (2014) 'Focus on landscapes', 83.

Steel, B. 'Physical geography – primary', GTIP Think Piece www.geography.org.uk/gtip/thinkpieces/physical geography(primary)/#1465

Other useful links

www.nsead.org

www.takeonepicture.org